THE LAST TRUMPET

THE LAST TRUMPET

CHRIST'S RETURN AND THE AWAKENING OF A SLEEPING CHURCH
A PROPHETIC CRY TO ROUSE THE BRIDE BEFORE THE SKY SPLITS OPEN

DAMIANO B. CENTOLA

EXPLORA BOOKS
700 – 838 West Hastings St. Vancouver
BC V6C 0A6
www.explorabooks.com
Phone: (604) 330 6795

No part of this book may be reproduced, stored in a retrieval system, or transmitted by any means without the written permission of the author.

Because of the dynamic nature of the Internet, any web addresses or links contained in this book may have changed since publication and may no longer be valid. The views expressed in this work are solely those of the author and do not necessarily reflect the views of the publisher, and the publisher hereby disclaims any responsibility for them.

Bible verses are quoted from the King James Version (KJV), which is public domain, the English Standard Version (ESV), and the New King James Version (NKJV).

ISBN: 978-1-83430-060-3 *(Paperback)*
978-1-83430-061-0 *(Hardback)*
978-1-83430-062-7 *(eBook)*

© 2025 Damiano B. Centola. All rights reserved.

Dedication

To the ones who are watching,
To the Bride who still has oil in her lamp,
To the remnant who will not bow to Baal,
To the intercessors who groan for the return of the King,
To every saint who has dared to stand alone in a sleeping generation—
This is for you.
And to the One who is coming quickly,
Whose voice will shake the heavens and earth,
Whose eyes are as fire,
Whose robe is dipped in blood,
To Jesus Christ, the Faithful and True,
This trumpet sounds for You.

—Damiano B. Centola

Table of Contents

Dedication i
Preface v
Introduction vii
Chapter I The Sound of the Trumpet 1
Chapter II The Church Asleep in the Garden 7
Chapter III When the Bride Forgets the Groom 13
Chapter IV The Rise of False Glory and Falling Away 17
Chapter V The Final Harvest and the Cry of the Remnant 23
Chapter VI The Sky Splits Open: What the Prophets Saw 29
Chapter VII The Fiery Return of the King 35
Chapter VIII Judgment Begins at the House of God 41
Chapter IX What the Remnant Must Do Now 47
Chapter X The New Jerusalem and the Final Amen 53
Conclusion 57
Glossary of Biblical Terms 61
Scripture Index 65
Appendix 71
Acknowledgments 77
About the Author 79
Back Cover Blurb 81

Preface

There are moments in history when the whisper of God becomes a thunder. This is such a moment.

This book was not born from comfort or convenience. It came to life in the furnace of prayer, through sleepless nights and divine urgency. I did not choose to write it—I was summoned to declare it. The pages ahead are not merely commentary on prophecy; they are a trumpet call to a Church lulled into slumber, a Bride distracted by the world while the Bridegroom draws near.

For too long, the conversation around the return of Christ has either been silenced, sensationalized, or suffocated by theological disagreement. But now, the Spirit is pressing again—calling for a remnant that will rise, for watchmen who will not keep silent, for lamps trimmed with oil.

This is not a book about timelines and charts. It is about readiness. It is about intimacy with the One who is coming. It is about the cry that is echoing across the nations: "Behold, the Bridegroom cometh; go ye out to meet Him."

I write to those whose hearts burn, who sense the hour but are unsure how to prepare. I write to pastors, to prophets, to intercessors, to worshipers, to the hidden and the hungry. I write to the sleeping, in hopes that they will awaken. And I write to the ready, in hopes that they will warn others.

The time is short, the trumpet is sounding, and Heaven is not silent. May this book pierce, provoke, and prepare. For the King is not just coming—He is at the door.

— Damiano B. Centola

Introduction

The Last Trumpet: Christ's Return and the Awakening of a Sleeping Church— A prophetic cry to rouse the Bride before the sky splits open.

By Damiano B. Centola

> *Therefore be ye also ready: for in such an hour as ye think not the Son of man cometh."* — Matthew 24:44

The Church is not ready.

These words may unsettle some and offend others, but they are true. While many await a political savior or a financial revival, the Son of Man stands at the threshold, eyes ablaze, robe dipped in blood, with the armies of heaven behind Him. And yet, many of His people sleep. The lamps grow dim. The cry of the watchmen fades into the noise of culture. The Bride has grown distracted. The altar has grown cold.

This book is not about when Jesus will return—it is about how we are to live in light of His return. It is about the forgotten cry of the prophets, the neglected urgency of the apostles, and the holy fear that once gripped the early Church. It is a call to rediscover the trembling joy of the Blessed Hope.

For centuries, the second coming of Christ was the heartbeat of the Church. It produced martyrs, shaped nations, ignited revivals, and purified hearts. But in this generation, it has too often become a theological footnote or a cinematic spectacle. The trumpet has been muffled by entertainment. The urgency has been hijacked by apathy.

This must change.

We are nearing the moment when the heavens will break open, and the King of Glory will descend—not as a lamb to be slain, but as a lion to reign. And His eyes will search for faith. His reward will be with Him. His judgment will be final. There will be no warning bell—only the sound of a trumpet.

This book is a prophetic alarm to the slumbering Church. It is not a call to fear, but to fire. Not a summons to escape, but to endure. It is about repentance, watchfulness, holiness, and longing. It is about the cry of the Spirit and the Bride: "Come, Lord Jesus."

Prepare your heart. Strengthen your lamp. Wake the others.

He is coming.

— Damiano B. Centola

Chapter I
The Sound of the Trumpet

"Blow ye the trumpet in Zion, and sound an alarm in my holy mountain: let all the inhabitants of the land tremble: for the day of the LORD cometh, for it is nigh at hand."
— *Joel 2:1*

The trumpet is not a soft instrument. It does not whisper. It does not suggest. It declares. When heaven chooses a trumpet, it is not for ambiance—it is for awakening. In ancient Israel, the trumpet—called the shofar—was blown to announce war, declare feasts, gather the people, and signal the approach of divine visitation. It was never casual. It always demanded a response. And now, in this hour, the sound of the last trumpet is echoing once more—not through brass, but through prophets, preachers, dreams, visions, and anointed writings. The Spirit is sounding the alarm across a sleeping Bride.
We have reached a turning point in the history of man, and of the Church. Not the Church as she is labeled by denomination or structure, but the living Body of Christ scattered across the earth. Many in this Body have grown drowsy—lulled by ease, distracted by prosperity, and numbed by

compromise. But the trumpet is not concerned with comfort. The trumpet is concerned with readiness.

This chapter is not an attempt to decode the exact hour of Christ's return, but to awaken those with ears to hear that we are standing on the edge of eternity. The trumpet has already begun to blow.

The Trumpet and the Pattern of God

Throughout Scripture, God has used the trumpet to signal moments of transition and visitation. When Israel stood at the base of Mount Sinai, preparing to receive the Law, the trumpet of God grew louder and louder (*Exodus 19:16–19*). When Jericho was to fall, the people marched for seven days, and on the final day, seven trumpets blew—and the walls came crashing down (*Joshua 6:4–20*). When Gideon shattered the enemy's camp, it began with the blast of a trumpet and the breaking of a vessel (*Judges 7:19–22*).

The trumpet is a divine pattern. It signals a breaking point—when God moves to confront sin, shift nations, or visit His people in glory or judgment.

So what does it mean that the last trumpet is sounding? What are we being called to awaken to?

Not the End of the World—The End of the Delay

Many today ask, "Is it the end of the world?" But the better question is, "Is this the end of God's silence?" For there is a silence before the trumpet—a period when heaven waits, when prayers are stored in bowls, and justice tarries while mercy pleads. But once the trumpet sounds, the delay is over. The scrolls are opened. The King stands up. What was long-patient is now urgent.

We are not at the end of time—we are at the end of delay.

This is not merely about the second coming in theology—it is about the second coming in reality. It is about preparing for the return of Christ not just in eschatological theory but in bridal urgency.

The Trumpet and the Church Today

Today's Church is saturated with conferences, content, convenience—and yet we lack clarity. We have filled our calendars, yet many pulpits are silent about the one event that every apostle longed for: the return of the King. The early Church preached it as a hope and a warning. They expected His return. They lived for it. Died for it. Kept themselves pure for it.

But in our day, many have traded the trumpet for a flute—soothing the masses rather than sounding the alarm. We are entertaining saints instead of enlisting soldiers. The trumpet is not for performance—it is for preparation. He is coming. And every true believer must feel the weight of that declaration. Not to fear, but to focus. Not to panic, but to purify.

The Trumpet in You

There is a trumpet within every believer that the Holy Spirit longs to awaken. It is the call to live watchfully, to pray fervently, to burn brightly. It is the call to repent of dullness and arise in expectation. This is not a generation to spectate—it is a generation to participate in the greatest unfolding of God's glory in human history.

The trumpet does not ask for perfection. It demands response.

Will you rise to meet Him?

Will you trim your lamp?

Will you shake off slumber?

He is not coming for the tired, but the trimmed.

Not for the distracted, but the devoted.

Not for the churchgoer, but for the Bride.

A Call to Respond

The trumpet has never been about noise—it's about notice. It is heaven saying, "The time has come. Prepare yourself. The King approaches." And so, as we begin this journey, let this first chapter not merely be information—but impartation. The alarm is sounding. The Spirit is speaking. The heavens are stirring.

Let the Bride awaken.

Let the watchmen cry out.

Let the remnant prepare.

For the trumpet of the Lord is blowing, and the sky is about to open.

Chapter II
The Church Asleep in the Garden

"And he cometh unto the disciples, and findeth them asleep, and saith unto Peter, What, could ye not watch with me one hour? Watch and pray, that ye enter not into temptation: the spirit indeed is willing, but the flesh is weak."

— *Matthew 26:40–41*

The night was heavy. The hour dark. The Savior, trembling in agony, poured out His soul beneath the olive trees. Just feet away, the disciples slept. The contrast is haunting. Heaven groaned while earth slumbered. Christ watched in anguish while His followers collapsed in fatigue.

And yet this image is more than a historical account—it is a prophetic mirror. The Church today is again in a garden moment. The final hour is upon us. Shadows stretch across the globe. The enemy plots. The cup is being passed. And while heaven shakes, the Church yawns. In many ways, we have repeated the same failure of Gethsemane: when called to watch, we slumbered. When asked to intercede, we entertained. When invited to stand, we sat.

This is not condemnation—it is a summons. The alarm is sounding to awaken a sleeping Bride.

A Prophetic Parallel

The Garden of Gethsemane was not merely a moment of sorrow—it was a test of spiritual alertness. Christ asked, "Could you not watch with me one hour?" It was not a question of effort, but of intimacy. To stay awake in this hour is to stay near to Him. Yet the disciples, like many of us, allowed fatigue to win the battle.

What kind of fatigue?

- Spiritual fatigue from constant distractions
- Emotional fatigue from constant compromise
- Doctrinal fatigue from watered-down teaching
- Moral fatigue from cultural pressure

The Church in many parts of the world is tired—not from persecution, but from overindulgence. We are asleep not because we've been beaten, but because we've been lulled.

The Danger of Drowsiness

Spiritual sleep is not simply inaction—it is unawareness. A sleeping Church loses discernment. It misses the signs of the times. It mistakes comfort for blessing. It tolerates what it should confront. When we slumber:

- We forget the urgency of the gospel
- We ignore the nearness of eternity
- We soften our message to suit modern ears
- We trade the oil of the Spirit for the applause of men

And so, while Jesus weeps over nations, many believers scroll endlessly. While the world spirals toward judgment, sermons avoid the topic. While the trumpet of His return grows louder, the Church looks for softer songs. This is not the hour to relax—it is the hour to rise.

The Call to Watch

Watching is not passive. It is active, alert, and urgent. Jesus commanded: "Watch and pray." Watching requires spiritual sensitivity. It means staying in the Word, living in communion, walking in holiness. It means asking:
- What is the Spirit saying to the churches?
- Where is God moving in this hour?
- How can I be found faithful, not comfortable?

In the early Church, to watch was to live with burning expectation. Paul lived like the trumpet could sound any moment. Peter wrote with urgency. John saw the heavens open and cried, "Even so, come, Lord Jesus." Somewhere along the way, we've lost that fire.

But the Holy Spirit is reigniting it.

The Awakening Begins in the Garden

Jesus did not scold His disciples in Gethsemane—He warned them. "Watch and pray… the spirit indeed is willing, but the flesh is weak." He knew they wanted to stay awake. He knows we want to please Him. But desire is not enough in this hour. We need discipline. We need holy focus. We need to cast off the drowsiness of distraction and take up the mantle of intercession.

The garden is not only a place of sorrow—it is the womb of revival. Jesus wrestled in prayer so that victory could be birthed. And He invites us to do the same.

The true awakening begins in the garden of intimacy.

For Such a Time as This

You were not born in this hour by accident. You were placed in the end times to shine, not to sleep. You were called to be part of the remnant that watches, that warns, that waits for His return with burning lamps and unshaken faith.

The Bridegroom is stirring. The fig tree is budding. The trumpet is warming. And yet… the Church is still in the garden.

Will we stay asleep?

Or will we rise and follow Him to Calvary… to glory… to the skies?

Awake, O sleeper. The hour has come.

Chapter III
When the Bride Forgets the Groom

"Nevertheless I have somewhat against thee, because thou hast left thy first love."

— Revelation 2:4

There is a grief in heaven that we scarcely understand on earth. It is not the grief of rejection from the lost, but the heartbreak of a Groom whose Bride has forgotten Him. The Church, once burning with devotion, now drifts into routine. The Bride of Christ, once dressed in readiness, now slumbers in apathy. This chapter is not an indictment—it is a divine plea. When Jesus described the kingdom in His parable of the ten virgins, He spoke prophetically of the Church's posture at the end of the age: "While the bridegroom tarried, they all slumbered and slept" (Matthew 25:5). All. Even the wise. There comes a time, just before the midnight cry, when even the faithful grow weary. But heaven's clock ticks louder now.

The tragedy is not merely forgetfulness—it is misplaced affection. Like Israel of old, we chase after foreign lovers, strange fires, and new gospels. We build altars to performance and entertainment. We decorate our sanctuaries, but leave the altar cold. We perfect sound and lighting, but forget the Light of the World. The Bride no longer trembles before the Groom—she scrolls, sings, and sleeps.

How did we get here?

The modern Church is overwhelmed with knowledge but underwhelmed by awe. We know the Scriptures, but not the flame behind them. We dissect prophecy, yet forget the One who is called "Faithful and True." The groom is coming, but we've grown comfortable with His delay. We've substituted intimacy with productivity, passion with programs, worship with performance.

We speak of revival, but we do not remember the Reviver.

In the first century, the early Church was not large, wealthy, or politically powerful, but she was pure. She walked in the fear of the Lord and the comfort of the Holy Spirit. Today, many churches boast size, status, and influence—but where is the trembling? Where is the fire on the altar? Where are the tears of longing?

The Symptoms of a Forgetful Bride

A Bride who forgets the Groom:

- Becomes enamored with herself.
- Measures her worth by applause, not by obedience.
- Replaces holiness with hype.
- Uses the gifts of the Spirit as ornaments rather than tools for edification.
- Chooses relevance over reverence.

This is not merely a moral crisis; it is a heart crisis.

Jesus is not coming back for a brilliant organization but for a burning lover. He is not betrothed to a corporation but to a people washed in the Word and wooed by His Spirit. He longs for a Bride who remembers His touch, who weeps over His absence, who waits with oil in her lamp.

A Call to Return

"Return, O backsliding children, saith the LORD; for I am married unto you" (Jeremiah 3:14).

This is the cry of a jealous God. He is not angry because we failed—He is grieved because we forgot.

Revival does not begin with noise. It begins with remembering.

Remembering who He is.

Remembering what He did.

Remembering why we said yes in the first place.

"Thou shalt remember the LORD thy God..." (Deuteronomy 8:18).

When memory is restored, so is mercy.

When remembrance returns, so does repentance.

And when repentance is true, love becomes holy again.

The Oil and the Cry

The parable ends with a midnight cry: "Behold, the bridegroom cometh!" But only half the virgins had oil. The others, too distracted to prepare, were locked out. Oil does not appear overnight. It is cultivated in the secret place. The Bride who remembers the Groom is the one who watches in the dark and waits in the Spirit.

There is still time to awaken. Still time to return. Still time to remember.

But not much.

Let the cry go forth: The Bridegroom is coming! Let the Bride make herself ready.

Not with glamor, but with garments of righteousness.

Not with power, but with purity.

Not with noise, but with nearness.

He remembers you.

Do you remember Him?

Chapter IV
The Rise of False Glory and Falling Away

"Let no man deceive you by any means: for that day shall not come, except there come a falling away first..."
— *2 Thessalonians 2:3*

We are living in a time when light shows in sanctuaries are mistaken for glory, and emotional highs are mistaken for revival. A generation hungry for spiritual experience has become vulnerable to spiritual deception. The rise of false glory always precedes the return of true glory, and the counterfeit always races ahead of the King to deceive the crowd.

This chapter is not for the curious—it is for the discerning. For the Spirit says expressly that in the last days many shall depart from the faith, giving heed to seducing spirits and doctrines of devils *(1 Timothy 4:1)*. The stage is set, the lights are blinding, and many do not see the exit sign flickering above the Church door. What is leaving us is not popularity—it is Presence.

The Golden Calf of the Modern Age

False glory is always shiny. It is always loud. It always draws a crowd.

It also always lacks the fire of holiness.

Just as Israel built a golden calf while Moses lingered on the mountain, so too does a modern Church build false altars when God tarries. We trade waiting for worshiptainment. We seek prophecy without repentance. We create platforms without prayer closets. And we boast of revival while the ark is missing.

The glory of God is not a feeling—it is a Person. His name is Holy. Where He is, there is trembling. Where He is, there is fire. Where He is, there is truth.

But where is the falling away?

It is not always loud. It is often subtle. It looks like:

- Churches without crosses.
- Sermons without repentance.
- Ministries that center on man, not Christ.
- Signs without submission.
- Crowds with no crucifixion of the flesh.

We are witnessing a quiet exodus—not from churches, but from truth. And as truth is forsaken, glory departs.

Ichabod in the House

In 1 Samuel 4, the ark of the covenant was captured, and the glory of God departed from Israel. The son born in that moment was named Ichabod—"the glory has departed." This was not a metaphor. It was a spiritual reality. God's presence was no longer with them, though the rituals remained.

Today, the Ichabod spirit is creeping into pulpits. The ark is replaced with stage fog. The lampstand flickers. But because the people still clap, no one notices that heaven is quiet.

The Seduction of Signs

Jesus warned that false prophets and false Christs would arise, performing great signs and wonders to deceive, if possible, even the elect (*Matthew 24:24*). The miracle alone is no longer a reliable measure. Pharaoh's magicians mimicked Moses 'signs. The antichrist will deceive the nations with signs.

True glory is not flashy—it is holy.
True revival does not entertain—it convicts.
True power does not elevate man—it reveals the Lamb.

The Spirit of Antichrist in the House of God

Paul warned that before the coming of the Lord, a "man of sin" would be revealed—exalting himself in the temple of God (*2 Thessalonians 2:4*). Many are looking for the antichrist in the political world, but few are discerning the antichrist spirit in the house of God.

This spirit:
- Replaces Christ-centered worship with self-centered platforms.
- Distorts grace into lawlessness.
- Falsifies spiritual gifts without fruit.
- Elevates emotion over truth.
- Rejects sound doctrine in favor of trending revelations.

This is the falling away—hidden behind bright stages, smooth words, and cleverly branded ministries. But Heaven sees it. And the remnant must sound the alarm.

Calling the Remnant to Discern

The falling away is not a singular event—it is a progressive seduction. The antidote is not panic, but discernment. Not fear, but fire.

We must:
- Return to the Word of God as our plumb line.
- Test every spirit by the Spirit.
- Anchor ourselves in the fear of the Lord.
- Guard our hearts from celebrity culture in the Church.
- Cry out for true glory—weighty, holy, refining fire.

Let the Church Weep Again

Until we weep over the false, we will not long for the true.

Until we groan again for His presence, we will settle for platforms.

Until we see the counterfeit for what it is, we will mistake noise for nearness.

The Bride must not be dazzled by the imitation.

She must long again for the real.

The trumpet is sounding, and judgment begins at the house of God. Let us cleanse our temples before the King arrives. Let the false glory be exposed, and let the Bride return to the fire.

Chapter V
The Final Harvest and the Cry of the Remnant

"Thrust in thy sickle, and reap: for the time is come for thee to reap; for the harvest of the earth is ripe."
— *Revelation 14:15*

There is a cry rising—not from stages or pulpits, but from caves, closets, and broken altars. It is not the voice of the popular, but of the prepared. It is the sound of the remnant—those few who have not bowed to Baal, who have not compromised under pressure, and who burn for the return of the King. The fields are white, the end is near, and the Bride must awaken for the final harvest.

This is not a harvest of casual converts. It is a harvest of hearts shaken, stirred, and sanctified. It is the last wave before the wind changes. The voice of the Spirit is calling: "Prepare ye the way of the Lord."

The Urgency of the Hour

The hour is late. The darkness is thick. Yet the light of the remnant burns brighter than ever. While many sleep, a few are sowing. While many play, a few are planting in tears. And while the world scrolls, heaven watches—for the time has come for the sickle to swing.

This is not the time for lukewarm love or half-hearted missions. The cry of the remnant must match the urgency of the throne.

The night is far spent, the day is at hand." — Romans 13:12

There is no more time for ego-driven ministry or entertainment-focused churches. We must shift from comfort to commission. From spectators to sowers. From apathy to agony for souls.

The Remnant: Few, Faithful, and Flaming

Throughout redemptive history, God has always used a remnant. Noah in a corrupt world. Elijah on Mount Carmel. Jeremiah in a decaying nation. John in the wilderness. And today—He calls again.

The remnant is:

- Small in number but great in fire.
- Hidden from fame but known in heaven.
- Unmoved by culture and married to the cross.

They do not care for applause. They seek His appearing.

"And they that be wise shall shine as the brightness of the firmament..." — Daniel 12:3

The remnant weeps where others laugh. They intercede while others sleep. They carry oil in their lamps and tremble at His Word. They cry out in the Spirit, "Lord, not one soul be lost!"

The Call to Travail

Before there is reaping, there is groaning. Paul wrote, "My little children, of whom I travail in birth again until Christ be formed in you…" (*Galatians 4:19*). Travail is not just prayer—it is a deep cry from the Spirit, groaning for souls.

Who will groan for this generation?
Who will weep for the next?
Who will stand between the porch and the altar and cry, "Spare Thy people, O Lord"?
The remnant is not impressive—they are intercessors.
This final harvest requires:
- Tears on the altar.
- Knees on the floor.
- Eyes on eternity.

It is not about programs. It is about presence.
It is not about movements. It is about the Man—Christ Jesus, returning in power.

Reaping with the Sickle of Truth
The Word of God is the sickle.
The Spirit of God is the wind.
The saints of God are the workers in the field.
The harvest is not just numbers—it is names written in the Lamb's Book of Life.
We must preach truth again—uncut, unedited, and full of fire.
We must love like Christ—bold, broken, and burdened for souls.
We must move in power—marked by humility and holiness.
There is no other time but now.
There is no other name but His.
There is no other harvest after this.

He that goeth forth and weepeth, bearing precious seed, shall doubtless come again with rejoicing..." — Psalm 126:6

The Trumpet and the Sickle

The trumpet is sounding. The sickle is swinging. Heaven and hell are watching. What will we do?

Will we sleep while the fields rot?

Will we entertain while the end draws near?

Or will we rise as laborers, burning with glory, weeping for souls, and running to the fields?

Let the remnant rise.

Let the trumpet awaken.

Let the harvest begin.

Chapter VI
The Sky Splits Open: What the Prophets Saw

"And then shall appear the sign of the Son of man in heaven... and they shall see the Son of man coming in the clouds of heaven with power and great glory."
— Matthew 24:30

From the ancient scrolls of Ezekiel to the final visions of John on Patmos, the prophets spoke of a moment that would shatter time itself—a divine rupture in the fabric of the sky. This was not poetic exaggeration, but prophetic vision: a literal, visible, cosmic unveiling. Heaven opens. Earth trembles. The King returns.

The prophets didn't speak in riddles to amuse the religious. They thundered with holy fire to prepare the faithful. What they saw was not symbolic alone—it was terrifying, glorious, and imminent.

Ezekiel Saw the Wheels

Ezekiel, by the river Chebar, saw visions that many dismissed as mystical or unknowable. But through the storm and the fire, he described wheels within wheels, full of eyes, moving with living creatures in perfect unity (*Ezekiel 1*).

This was not abstract art—it was throne-chariot theology. He saw the mobile majesty of God. And that same glory Ezekiel saw departing the temple would one day descend again—not as warning, but as return.

> *And, behold, the glory of the God of Israel came from the way of the east..." — Ezekiel 43:2*

Ezekiel saw the glory depart—and he saw it return. The King is coming back, not to visit—but to reign.

Daniel Saw the Son of Man

Daniel, the prophet of kingdoms and beasts, peered through time to see thrones set in place and the Ancient of Days seated. But more strikingly, he saw:

> *One like the Son of Man coming with the clouds of heaven."*
> *— Daniel 7:13*

Daniel didn't see a symbolic movement—he saw a Man. A divine-human King, riding on clouds, approaching the throne, receiving everlasting dominion. This is not mythology. This is Messiah.

He saw the second coming of Christ long before Bethlehem, long before Calvary. And it burned in his bones.

Zechariah Saw Him Pierced

Zechariah, prophet of the post-exile restoration, saw something stunning:

> *And they shall look upon me whom they have pierced..."*
> *— Zechariah 12:10*

He foresaw a time when Israel would behold their once-rejected King—pierced, but returning. Not meek and lowly. But glorious and sovereign.

The second coming is not vague. The prophets were not confused. They saw Him: pierced, returning, triumphant.

John Saw the Sky Rip Open

John, the beloved disciple, exiled to Patmos, was lifted into the realm of eternal vision. And he wrote:

And I saw heaven opened, and behold a white horse; and He that sat upon him was called Faithful and True..."
— Revelation 19:11

Heaven opened—not symbolically, but physically. John saw the sky split. He saw the return of Jesus—not as a baby, not as a lamb, but as the rider on the white horse, clothed in a robe dipped in blood, leading heaven's armies. The second coming is not a whisper. It is a war cry.

What Does It Mean for Us?

If the prophets saw it…
If the Word confirms it…
If the sky will split and He will return…
Then we must live ready.
This means:
- Eyes on the clouds, not the chaos.
- Hearts on fire, not distracted.
- Lives in alignment, not drifting.

The second coming will not be a secret event. It will be the loudest, most visible, and most decisive moment in human history. Every eye will see Him. Every knee will bow. Every tongue will confess.

Will you be found waiting or wandering?

This Is Not a Drill

Too many sermons soften this moment. Too many songs romanticize it. But the sky splitting is holy, fearful, and final.

It is the end of the age. The end of compromise. The end of time as we know it.

It is also the beginning of glory for those who are His.

Let the church preach this again. Let pulpits thunder with the vision of His return. Let artists paint it, let poets write it, let prophets declare it:

He is coming.

The sky will split.

The King will descend.

And it will be exactly as the prophets said.

Chapter VII
The Fiery Return of the King

"...the Lord Jesus shall be revealed from heaven with His mighty angels, in flaming fire..."
— *2 Thessalonians 1:7–8*

He will not come back quietly.

His return will not resemble His first arrival—a fragile infant in a borrowed manger, veiled in obscurity and wrapped in humility. The next time He comes, the heavens will ignite. The elements will melt. The proud will tremble. And the faithful will rejoice.

This is not metaphor. This is Majesty.

The return of Christ will be fiery, final, and glorious—the decisive unveiling of the King of kings.

Fire as Judgment, Fire as Glory

In Scripture, fire represents both purification and punishment. For those who belong to Him, the fire is a purifier, a glory, a refining flame. For those who have rejected Him, it is terror. Paul writes:

> *"...taking vengeance on them that know not God, and that obey not the gospel of our Lord Jesus Christ."*
> *— 2 Thessalonians 1:8*

This is the fire of holy retribution—not spiteful, but righteous. The long-withheld wrath of God will pour out, not in chaos but in perfect justice. He comes not only to rescue the remnant but to judge the rebellious. The King's fire is not random—it is targeted, measured, and holy.

The Revelation of the Lamb as Lion

The first time He came, the Lamb was silent before His shearers. The second time, the Lion of Judah will roar.

> *Behold, the Lion of the tribe of Judah hath prevailed..."*
> *— Revelation 5:5*

He is no longer veiled. No longer hidden. The glory that was once glimpsed by Peter, James, and John on the Mount of Transfiguration will now cover the earth.

And all who mocked His delay will bow before His dominion.

This return is not partial. It is total. Not symbolic. It is cosmic.

Heaven's Army Rides With Him

He does not return alone. John saw it:

> *And the armies which were in heaven followed Him upon white horses, clothed in fine linen, white and clean."*
> *— Revelation 19:14*

Who are these armies? They are the redeemed. The saints. Those who overcame by the blood of the Lamb.

Heaven will not send an ambassador. It sends an army.

Because this is not a suggestion. It is a takeover.

Christ does not return to negotiate. He returns to reign.

His Robe Is Dipped in Blood

The image is graphic. Fearful. Holy.

> *And He was clothed with a vesture dipped in blood: and His name is called The Word of God."*
> *— Revelation 19:13*

This is not the blood of His crucifixion. It is the blood of His enemies. It is the manifestation of His role as the righteous Judge.

We cannot soften this.

We must not tame it.

He is both Savior and Judge, both Bridegroom and Warrior.

The same hands that healed lepers and lifted children now carry a sword. The voice that once calmed storms now commands angelic legions. And the One who once wept over Jerusalem now rides to rule the nations.

Every Eye Shall See Him

> *Behold, He cometh with clouds; and every eye shall see Him..."*
> *— Revelation 1:7*

This is not spiritual only. This is literal. Global. Undeniable.

From the cities of the West to the deserts of the East, from the mountain tribes to the technocratic towers—every soul will see Him. The digital age will not obscure Him. The skeptics will not ignore Him.

The sun will dim before His brilliance.

The earth will reel before His steps.

And the King will return.

What Does This Demand of Us?

This is not a scene to merely observe. It is a truth that demands response.

- Live as though He could come today.
- Preach as if fire is about to fall.
- Repent while the door is still open.
- Worship with awe.
- Watch with readiness.

The fiery return of the King is the culmination of history—the moment that every prophet pointed toward and every saint has longed for.

It is the blessed hope of the Church.

It is the terror of the godless.

It is the glory of the Kingdom.

When He returns, there will be no more debate.

Only worship or wailing.

The King is coming—and this time, He brings fire.

Chapter VIII
Judgment Begins at the House of God

"For the time is come that judgment must begin at the house of God..."
— *1 Peter 4:17*

Long before the sword strikes Babylon, it swings through the sanctuary.
Before the world is judged in fire, the Church is judged in truth.
The sobering truth of Scripture is this: God cleanses His house before He conquers the nations. His love demands it. His holiness commands it. His justice enforces it.
This is not condemnation—it is correction. Not destruction—but refinement.
And yet, the Church today often thinks judgment is only for "them." The evil ones. The pagans. The wicked systems of the world.
But the Word says otherwise:

"If it first begin at us, what shall the end be of them that obey not the gospel of God?" — **1 Peter 4:17**

God is not coming to affirm our performances.
He is coming to purify His people.

The Temple Must Be Cleansed

When Jesus first entered the Temple in Jerusalem, He didn't sit quietly or give a motivational speech.

He turned over tables.

He drove out money changers.

He cleansed His Father's house.

That same zeal still burns in His eyes.

What does He see now in His Church?

- Pulpits compromised for popularity
- Sanctuaries more concerned with style than Spirit
- Leaders driven by ego, not eternity
- Saints entertained but not equipped

The whip is in His hand again—not out of rage, but out of righteous jealousy. He will have a Bride without blemish.

He is not coming for a sleeping, sulking, or straying Church. He is coming for a pure and prepared Bride.

Prophets Are Arising, But So Is Fire

In this hour, true prophets cry out:

"Repent, Church. Purify your altars. Remove the mixture."

Not all judgment is final. Some is merciful.

God sends correction now so we won't be condemned later.

The fire of judgment that begins in the house of God is not meant to destroy the house—it is meant to restore it.

- It burns off false doctrine.
- It exposes hidden sin.
- It dismantles prideful towers.
- It sifts the wheat from the chaff.

Revival will not come through compromise. It will only come through cleansing.

Accountability in the Priesthood

Ezekiel 9 reveals a terrifying vision: judgment begins at the sanctuary—with the elders, the priests.

> *"Begin at My sanctuary."* — *Ezekiel 9:6*

Those who were supposed to lead in holiness had grown numb to sin. God did not skip over them. He started with them.

In this hour, spiritual leaders are not exempt—they are first in line. The higher the call, the greater the weight of accountability.

Shepherds who have fed themselves instead of the flock...
Prophets who prophesied for gain instead of truth...
Worship leaders who performed but did not tremble...
He is coming to purify the priesthood.

The Remnant Will Shine in the Fire

To the faithful, this judgment is not punishment—it is promotion. It is the testing of gold in the furnace. It is the pruning of fruitful vines so they may bear more fruit.

Those who have not bowed to Baal...
Those who still preach Christ crucified...
Those who tremble at His Word...
They will emerge from the fire radiant, refined, and ready.

> *Then shall the righteous shine forth as the sun in the kingdom of their Father."* — *Matthew 13:43*

The fire that scorches the surface also reveals the root.

The Final Warning to the Lukewarm

Laodicea was not judged for outright rebellion. It was judged for lukewarmness.

> *Because thou art lukewarm... I will spue thee out of My mouth."*
> *— Revelation 3:16*

This is not a verse for the secular world. It is for the Church.

It is for the Christian who confesses Christ but lives in compromise.

It is for the pastor who preaches grace but never calls for repentance.

It is for the church that loves relevance more than reverence.

Jesus stands at the door of His own Church—knocking. Not to visit. To take over.

The House Must Be in Order

Before the trumpet sounds and the sky opens...

Before the King returns and the nations are judged...

Before the wrath is poured out on Babylon...

The Church must be made ready.

The house of God must be set in order.

Because the Lord is coming—not just to His Church... but through it.

Will He find us faithful?

> *They that understand among the people shall instruct many..."*
> *— Daniel 11:33*

Chapter IX
What the Remnant Must Do Now

"And they that be wise shall shine as the brightness of the firmament; and they that turn many to righteousness as the stars for ever and ever."
— *Daniel 12:3*

There is a people rising—not loud, not proud, not platformed—but pure, pierced, and prepared.
They are the remnant.
Not the majority, but the mighty.
Not the trendy, but the tried.
Not the loudest in the room, but the deepest in the Spirit.
They are awakened, alert, and aligned with the King.
And they know: this is the hour to move.
So what must the remnant do—now, before the sky splits, before the Bridegroom returns?

1. Return to the Secret Place

Not to events.

Not to personalities.

Not even to platforms.

But to the closet. The hidden chamber. The furnace of divine encounter.

> *When thou prayest, enter into thy closet..."*
>
> — *Matthew 6:6*

The secret place is where power returns. Where perspective is refined. Where fire falls.

The sleeping Church must become a watching Bride again—lamps trimmed, oil stocked, ears tuned to the whisper of God.

2. Purge the Mixture

No revival will come without repentance.

No glory will descend where idols are protected.

We must rid ourselves of every hybrid gospel, every compromised message, every unclean alliance.

> *Come out from among them, and be ye separate, saith the Lord..."*
>
> — *2 Corinthians 6:17*

This is not legalism. It is loyalty.

Holiness is not a restriction—it is a requirement for the vessels that will carry the coming glory.

3. Proclaim the Full Gospel—Without Shame

In an age where many dilute the truth to be accepted, the remnant will declare the truth to set captives free.

Not watered-down. Not politically safe. Not seeker-friendly. But Spirit-filled.

> *Woe unto me, if I preach not the gospel!"* — *1 Corinthians 9:16*

We must preach repentance and resurrection. Holiness and healing. The blood, the cross, the kingdom, and the King.

And we must not flinch.

4. Disciple the Few Who Will Go Deep

The call is not to entertain the masses, but to equip the remnant.

- Teach them the Word.
- Train them in prayer.
- Impart the fear of the Lord.
- Prepare them for persecution and glory.

We are not building crowds—we are preparing soldiers.

And soldiers are trained in secret, not in stadiums.

5. Weep Between the Porch and the Altar

Let the priests, the ministers of the Lord, weep..." — Joel 2:17

Intercession must rise.

Not passive. Not poetic. But priestly.

- Crying out for mercy.
- Groaning for nations.
- Warring in the Spirit for the Bride to awaken.

The remnant knows: the altar is not an accessory—it is the battlefield.

6. Stand Unshaken in the Midst of Shaking

The earth will tremble. Systems will collapse. Darkness will increase.

But the remnant will not be moved.

They shall not be ashamed in the evil time: and in the days of famine they shall be satisfied." — Psalm 37:19

Their anchor is not culture—it is Christ.

Their strength is not strategy—it is Spirit.

Their security is not money—it is the Messiah.

7. Sound the Alarm—Wake the Others

Blow ye the trumpet in Zion, and sound an alarm in my holy mountain..." — Joel 2:1

We are not only being prepared—we are being sent.

To warn.

To watch.

To woo the sleeping Bride with the urgency of eternity.

The sky is not silent. The trumpet is near. The Master is rising from His throne.

Now is the time to speak with holy fire, not soft whispers.

A People Without Mixture Will See His Glory

The remnant will be few, but they will be filled.

Filled with the Spirit.

Filled with wisdom.

Filled with fire.

> *Arise, shine; for thy light is come..." — Isaiah 60:1*

Let others play church.

Let others flirt with darkness.

Let others argue about timelines.

We must burn. We must build. We must bow.

Because the King is coming. And the Bride must be ready.

Chapter X
The New Jerusalem and the Final Amen

"And I John saw the holy city, new Jerusalem, coming down from God out of heaven, prepared as a bride adorned for her husband."
— *Revelation 21:2*

All of time is building toward this moment.
Not merely the return of Christ—glorious as that is.
But the unveiling of a city, a bride, and a forever Kingdom where God dwells with man.
This is the final Amen. The restoration of all things. The climax of the story that began in a Garden and ends in a glorious City.
Let the skeptics mock. Let the nations rage. Let the powers tremble.
Heaven is coming down.

1. The City Not Made With Human Hands

The New Jerusalem is not a renovated earthly empire. It is not built by political alliances or religious efforts.

It is a divine reality, descending from the heart of God Himself.

> *Prepared as a bride adorned for her husband."*
> *— Revelation 21:2*

Its brilliance surpasses all imagination:

- Walls of jasper.
- Foundations of precious stones.
- Gates of single pearls.
- Streets of transparent gold.

But its true glory is not architectural—it is relational.

> *Behold, the tabernacle of God is with men..."*
> *— Revelation 21:3*

He will walk among us again—not as a veiled Savior, but as the King unveiled.

2. No More Tears, No More Night

This is the longing of every aching soul:

> *And God shall wipe away all tears from their eyes..."*
> *— Revelation 21:4*

No more death.

No more sorrow.

No more crying.

No more pain.

All that the curse brought—vanquished. All that sin stole—restored.

Heaven is not just a place of beauty. It is a place of healing. A place where eternity kisses every scar, and time no longer steals what matters most.

3. The Lamb Is the Light

In this City, there is no temple—for the Lord God Almighty and the Lamb are the temple.

There is no sun—for the glory of God illuminates it.

There is no night—for His presence never fades.

> *The Lamb is the light thereof."* — *Revelation 21:23*

What we saw in glimpses—in the tabernacle, the temple, the upper room—we now live in fully.

Unbroken worship.

Eternal radiance.

Face-to-face communion.

This is not the end. This is the beginning of all we were ever made for.

4. A Bride Prepared

The City is not just a place—it is a people.

> *Come hither, I will shew thee the bride, the Lamb's wife."*
> — *Revelation 21:9*

It is the purified Church. The victorious remnant. The overcoming saints, washed in the blood, refined by the fire, faithful to the end.

She is not stained.

She is not ashamed.

She is not silent.

She shines with the glory of her King.

5. The River and the Tree

From the throne flows a river of life.

On its banks grow the tree of life, bearing twelve fruits, one for each month, and leaves for the healing of nations.

> *And there shall be no more curse..."* — *Revelation 22:3*

The nations once divided, wounded, and at war—healed.

The languages once confused—united in praise.

The longing once buried—fulfilled in the presence of the Lamb.

This is not myth. This is not metaphor.
This is home.

6. Come, Lord Jesus

John, the beloved disciple, hears it again:

Behold, I come quickly..." — Revelation 22:12

And what is the cry of the Spirit and the Bride?

Not delay.

Not hesitation.

Even so, come, Lord Jesus." — Revelation 22:20

This is the final Amen—not just a word, but a wedding cry.

The Church, once drowsy and distracted, is now dressed and discerning.

The trumpet has sounded.

The fire has fallen.

The King is returning.

And the Bride is ready.

The Final Amen

He will come in fire—but will dwell in forever light.

He will judge the wicked—but will wipe the tears of the righteous.

He will restore all things—and nothing shall separate us from Him again.

Not height.

Not depth.

Not tribulation.

Not famine.

Not sword.

Nothing.

Amen. Come, Lord Jesus." — Revelation 22:20

And this is the cry of the book, of the Church, and of every burning heart:

Even so, come.

Conclusion

The Cry That Echoes Beyond Time
He which testifieth these things saith, Surely I come quickly. Amen. Even so, come, Lord Jesus."— Revelation 22:20
The trumpet has not yet sounded its last note.
The Bridegroom has not yet stepped through the veil.
The sky, though it shimmers with signs, has not yet torn open.
But the moment is near.
This is not the end of a book—it is the stirring of the final awakening.
Not an ending, but a summons.
Not a period, but a trumpet blast waiting to be answered.
This book was never written to be shelved.
It was written to be felt, wept over, and acted upon.

The Church Must Rise
This is the hour when slumber must break.
When oil must be purchased.
When lamps must be lit.
When altars must burn again with holy fire.
The Church does not wait for signs—she is the sign.
The Church does not watch in fear—she stands in faith.
The Church does not retreat—she readies herself.
Because He is not coming for a bride unsure of her love.
He is not returning for a Church half-awake.
He is coming for those who are watching, waiting, burning.

He Comes for the Remnant

There is a sound only the remnant will hear.

A trumpet call not echoed in earthly frequencies.

A cry that awakens the deep places—the holy longing—the groaning within the Bride:

> *The Spirit and the bride say, Come."— Revelation 22:17*

The remnant does not seek safety.

She seeks Him.

The remnant is not afraid of the shaking.

She is formed in it.

The remnant knows the hour.

She hears the hoofbeats.

She lives between the altar and the sky.

The Final Plea: Get Ready

If ever there was a time to repent, it is now.

If ever there was a time to return, it is now.

If ever there was a time to stand, to speak, to kneel, to fast, to worship—

It is now.

He is not delaying.

He is not silent.

He is not distant.

He is coming.

The question is not if, but who will be ready.

Let the Bride Say Come

Let every page in this book become a prayer.

Let every truth become a torch.

Let every whisper become a war cry.

And let the Bride of Christ rise and say:

> *Even so, come, Lord Jesus."*

For the King is mounted.
The sky is cracking.
The voice is echoing through eternity.
The Groom is near.
And the final Amen belongs to those who are ready.

Glossary of Biblical Terms

Altar Call

A summons to repentance, surrender, and commitment, traditionally made at the conclusion of a sermon, but here referring to the final prophetic invitation before Christ's return.

Antichrist

A prophesied end-times figure who will oppose God, deceive the nations, and exalt himself as divine. A counterfeit messiah.

(See 2 Thessalonians 2:3–4)

Apostasy

The falling away or rebellion against true faith. A spiritual defection, especially among those who once professed to follow Christ.

(See 1 Timothy 4:1)

Bride of Christ

The Church in her pure, faithful, and watchful identity—those who are spiritually betrothed to Jesus and prepared for His return.

(See Revelation 19:7–9)

Day of the Lord

A prophetic phrase referring to the time of God's final judgment and the Second Coming of Christ, marked by both glory for the righteous and wrath for the wicked.

(See Joel 2:1, Zephaniah 1:14–18)

End Times

The final era of human history prior to Christ's return, characterized by increased deception, tribulation, signs in nature, global unrest, and the purifying of the Church. *(See Matthew 24)*

Falling Away

A mass turning from truth and holiness in the last days—apostasy on a global or Church-wide scale. *(See 2 Thessalonians 2:3)*

Judgment

The divine evaluation of every soul and every nation, culminating in reward or punishment. It begins with God's own house *(1 Peter 4:17)* and ends before the Great White Throne. *(See Revelation 20:11–15)*

Kingdom of God

The sovereign rule and reign of God, both spiritual and physical, already breaking into the world through Christ, and yet to be fully consummated at His return. *(See Luke 17:20–21; Revelation 11:15)*

Last Trumpet

A prophetic signal of Christ's return, resurrection of the righteous, and the unfolding of final judgment. It is the climactic sound that splits history. *(See 1 Corinthians 15:52)*

Remnant

The faithful few who remain true to God in times of widespread compromise or persecution. The prophetic community that hears, prepares, and responds. *(See Romans 11:5; Revelation 12:17)*

Return of Christ (Second Coming)

The visible, bodily return of Jesus to the earth in glory, power, and judgment. Not a secret rapture, but a cosmic event that will shake heaven and earth. *(See Revelation 1:7; Matthew 24:30)*

Revival

A sovereign move of God marked by repentance, holiness, renewal, and the outpouring of the Holy Spirit. Often precedes awakening or harvest.

The Sleeping Church

A symbolic term for the modern Church that has grown dull, distracted, or spiritually unaware of the hour. Like the disciples in Gethsemane, she is being called to awaken.

The Sky Splits Open

A prophetic phrase indicating the visible unveiling of Christ at His return, when the heavens open and He comes with armies of angels.

(See Revelation 19:11)

Watchman

A spiritual guardian or prophetic voice who discerns the times, warns of danger, and calls the people to readiness.

(See Ezekiel 33:6–7)

White Throne Judgment

The final judgment of all mankind, where each is judged according to their deeds and their names in the Book of Life.

(See Revelation 20:11–15)

Scripture Index

Old Testament

Genesis

3:15 — The Seed of the Woman and the promise of redemption

6:5–7 — Judgment in the days of Noah

Exodus

12:12 — God's judgment on Egypt's gods

19:16–19 — The trumpet at Mount Sinai

Deuteronomy

4:30 — Tribulation and return to the Lord

30:6 — The circumcision of the heart in the last days

1 Kings

18:21 — Elijah confronts wavering Israel

2 Kings

2:11 — Elijah's heavenly ascent

Psalm

2:1–12 — The nations rage against the Anointed

24:7–10 — The King of Glory shall come in

50:3–6 — God comes with fire

89:14 — Justice and righteousness as foundation of His throne

96:13 — He shall judge the earth in truth

103:19 — His throne is in the heavens

126:5 — Those who sow in tears shall reap in joy

Isaiah

5:20 — Woe to those who call evil good

6:1–8 — Isaiah's vision of the Lord

13:9–13 — The day of the Lord's fierce anger

21:11 — The watchman's cry: "What of the night?"

24:19–23 — Earth reels, sky splits, Lord reigns

26:9 — When judgments are in the earth

30:30 — The Lord's voice and His fiery indignation

40:3–5 — Prepare the way of the Lord

52:7–10 — He will return to Zion

53:1–12 — The suffering Servant

60:1–2 — Darkness and glory arise together

63:1–6 — Messiah trampling the winepress alone

66:15–16 — Fire and sword in judgment

Jeremiah

6:10–19 — The people reject the watchman's warning

23:16–22 — False prophets and dreams

Ezekiel

3:17 — Watchman warning the house of Israel

7:5–9 — The end has come

33:1–11 — The duty of the watchman

36:26 — A new heart and spirit

Daniel

2:44 — The everlasting Kingdom

7:13–14 — The Son of Man receives dominion

12:1–3 — Resurrection and the time of the end

Joel

2:1–32 — Blow the trumpet in Zion

3:14 — Multitudes in the valley of decision

Amos

3:7 — God reveals secrets to His prophets

8:11 — A famine of hearing the word

Habakkuk

2:3 — The vision waits for an appointed time

3:3–6 — The Lord comes in glory

Zechariah

9:9–10 — The King comes in humility and reigns

12:10 — They shall look upon Him whom they pierced

14:4 — His feet shall stand on the Mount of Olives

Malachi

3:1–3 — The Messenger prepares the way

4:1–6 — The day of the Lord and return of Elijah

New Testament

Matthew

3:2 — "Repent, for the kingdom is at hand"

5:13–16 — Salt and light

7:21–23 — Depart from Me, I never knew you

10:22 — Hated for His name's sake

24:3–44 — Signs of the end and Christ's return

25:1–13 — Parable of the Ten Virgins

26:40–41 — Disciples asleep in Gethsemane

28:6 — "He is not here; He is risen"

Mark

13:26–37 — Coming in the clouds, stay awake

Luke

12:35–40 — Be ready for the Son of Man

17:26–30 — As in the days of Noah and Lot

18:8 — "Will He find faith on the earth?"

21:25–36 — Signs and the coming of the Son of Man

John

1:14 — The Word became flesh

10:27 — "My sheep hear My voice"

14:3 — "I will come again"

17:17 — "Thy Word is truth"

Acts

1:11 — "This same Jesus shall come again"

2:17–21 — In the last days, I will pour out My Spirit

17:31 — He has appointed a day to judge

Romans

11:5 — A remnant according to grace

13:11 — Now is the time to wake from sleep

1 Corinthians

15:51–52 — The last trumpet, resurrection

16:22 — "Maranatha!"

2 Corinthians

5:10 — We must all appear before the judgment seat

Galatians

1:6–9 — Another gospel brings a curse

Ephesians

5:14 — Awake, sleeper, and arise from the dead

Philippians

2:10–11 — Every knee shall bow

1 Thessalonians

4:16–17 — The Lord descends with a shout

5:1–6 — The day comes as a thief in the night

2 Thessalonians

2:3–10 — The falling away and man of sin

1 Timothy

4:1 — Some shall depart from the faith

2 Timothy

3:1–5 — Perilous times shall come

4:1–8 — Preach the word; love His appearing

Titus

2:13 — Blessed hope and glorious appearing

Hebrews

9:28 — Christ shall appear a second time

10:31 — It is fearful to fall into the hands of God

12:26–29 — Yet once more I shake heaven and earth

James

5:7–9 — The Judge is at the door

1 Peter

1:13 — Hope to the end

4:17 — Judgment begins at the house of God

2 Peter

3:3–13 — The day of the Lord comes as a thief

1 John

2:18 — Many antichrists have come

3:2–3 — We shall be like Him

4:1 — Test the spirits

Revelation

1:7 — He comes with clouds, every eye shall see

2–3 — Letters to the seven churches

6:12–17 — Sixth seal and wrath of the Lamb

11:15 — The kingdoms become Christ's

14:14–20 — The harvest of the earth

16:15 — "Behold, I come as a thief"

19:11–16 — Christ returns with fire and armies

20:11–15 — The Great White Throne judgment

21:1–8 — New heaven and new earth

22:12–20 — "Behold, I come quickly"

Appendix

A. Understanding the Terms: Key Biblical Distinctions

1.) Second Coming vs Rapture
- Rapture (*1 Thessalonians 4:16–17*) refers to the sudden catching away of believers to meet Christ in the air.
- Second Coming (*Revelation 19:11–16*) refers to Christ returning with His saints to rule and judge the earth.

2.) The Day of the Lord
A period in which God intervenes dramatically in human history to execute judgment and bring deliverance
(*Isaiah 13:9, Joel 2:31, 2 Peter 3:10*).

3.) The Remnant
The faithful few preserved through apostasy and judgment (*Romans 11:5, Revelation 14:12*). These are those who "follow the Lamb wherever He goes."

4.) The Bride of Christ
The collective body of true believers who remain faithful, pure, and prepared for Christ's return (*Revelation 19:7–9, Ephesians 5:27*).

B. Historical Trumpets in Scripture

1. Trumpet at Mount Sinai – Exodus 19:16–19 Signaled the descent of God and His voice.
2. Trumpets in Battle – Joshua 6:4–5 Used to bring down the walls of Jericho.
3. Feast of Trumpets – Leviticus 23:23–25 A memorial and prophetic shadow of awakening and warning.
4. The Last Trumpet – 1 Corinthians 15:52 Signals resurrection and transformation of believers.

C. Patterns of Sleep and Awakening in Scripture

1. Adam – Put to sleep to bring forth a bride (*Genesis 2:21*)
2. Samson – Fell asleep on Delilah's lap, lost strength (*Judges 16:19*)
3. Jonah – Asleep during storm (*Jonah 1:5*)
4. Disciples – Slept in Gethsemane during Christ's agony (*Matthew 26:40–41*)
5. Ten Virgins – All slept, only five had oil (*Matthew 25:1–13*)
6. Lesson: Sleep is not always sin, but unpreparedness is fatal.

D. Typology of the Return

Throughout Scripture, the Second Coming of Christ is prefigured in vivid, prophetic shadows—types that point forward to His glorious and final return. These are not coincidences or creative interpretations, but God-ordained symbols, woven into the sacred story of redemption to stir holy anticipation. These types, when unveiled, help the Bride understand the nature, urgency, and mystery of His return.

1. Noah's Ark — The Door of Salvation Before the Storm

In the days of Noah, judgment was coming, but salvation was offered through one ark, with only one door. Once that door was shut by God Himself, no one else could enter. This typifies Christ as the only Door (*John 10:9*), the singular ark of rescue before divine judgment floods the earth again—this time not by water, but by fire. The return of Christ will find many outside the ark, unaware that time has run out. As in the days of Noah, so shall it be in the days of the Son of Man (*Luke 17:26–27*).

2. Elijah's Fiery Chariot — The Sudden and Fiery Return

Elijah, the prophet of fire, did not taste death. Instead, he was caught up in a chariot of blazing glory, seen ascending into heaven by Elisha. His departure was sudden, supernatural, and visible. In the same manner, Jesus shall return from heaven in blazing fire (*2 Thessalonians 1:7–8*), with eyes like flames, riding not in secrecy, but in splendor. Elijah's chariot was a glimpse of the celestial invasion that will accompany the King's return.

3. The Jewish Wedding — The Bridegroom Comes at Midnight

In ancient Jewish tradition, a bride was chosen, betrothed, and prepared—but she never knew the precise hour when the bridegroom would return to claim her. He would come with a shout, often at midnight, and only those who were ready with oil in their lamps would enter the celebration. Jesus deliberately framed His return in this imagery (*Matthew 25:1–13*). The Second Coming is not only a royal procession but a bridal retrieval—the Bridegroom returning for a radiant and ready Church.

4. David's Return to Jerusalem — The Rejected King Comes to Reign

King David, though anointed, was exiled from his throne during the rebellion of Absalom. When the rebellion was over, David crossed the Jordan and was welcomed back by a remnant. This foreshadows Christ, the King rejected by His people, who will one day return to Jerusalem—crossing from the heavenly realm back to the Mount of Olives—to establish His kingdom with power and glory (*Zechariah 14:4; Revelation 11:15*). Like David, He comes not just to rule, but to reclaim what is His.

These typologies are not allegories—they are divine blueprints. They show us that history is not random, but prophetic. Every act of God in the past whispers of what is to come. Every page of Scripture pulses with the promise that He is coming again.

E. Prophetic Voices and the End-Time Church
- Isaiah – Spoke of the Holy One coming in fire (*Isaiah 66*)
- Jeremiah – Warned a stubborn people ignoring the trumpet (*Jeremiah 6:17*)
- Daniel – Saw the Son of Man receiving a kingdom (*Daniel 7*)
- Joel – Called for trumpet to awaken Zion (*Joel 2*)
- John the Revelator – Saw the sky split and the King return (*Revelation 19*)

F. Signs of His Coming
According to Matthew 24, Luke 21, and 2 Timothy 3, signs include:
- Wars and rumors of wars
- Famines, earthquakes, pestilences
- Deception and false prophets
- Great falling away
- Love growing cold
- Gospel preached to all nations
- The abomination of desolation
- Signs in the heavens
- Persecution of the righteous

G. Ancient Trumpets in Jewish Tradition
1. Tekiah – A long blast, signifying kingship
2. Shevarim – Three medium blasts, signifying brokenness
3. Teruah – Nine staccato blasts, a wake-up call
4. Tekiah Gedolah – The Great Blast, signifying final redemption

These sounds echo in heaven and foreshadow the coming King.

H. Ten Commandments for the Last Days Remnant
1. Watch and pray (*Luke 21:36*)
2. Remain sober and alert (*1 Thessalonians 5:6*)
3. Stay in the Word (*John 17:17*)
4. Do not love the world (*1 John 2:15*)
5. Discern the spirits (*1 John 4:1*)
6. Preach the gospel without shame (*Romans 1:16*)
7. Keep your lamp burning (*Luke 12:35*)
8. Be found faithful (*Matthew 24:46*)
9. Love His appearing (*2 Timothy 4:8*)
10. Live in holiness (*1 Peter 1:16*)

Acknowledgments

To write of the Second Coming is to tremble and weep at the threshold of eternity. This book was not born from study alone, but from prayer, tears, urgency, and a holy ache for the sleeping Church to arise.

First, I thank the Lord Jesus Christ, the soon-coming King. Every page is offered at Your feet. Every sentence bows to Your glory. May You find a bride burning when You return.

To the Holy Spirit, who breathed every line and stirred the trumpet in my spirit—thank You for the unrelenting conviction, comfort, and clarity. You are the Author behind the author.

To Feebe, my beloved wife, thank you for your unwavering intercession, your joy in the early mornings, and your strength beside me through the labor of this message. You carry the fire of the Bride, and your voice is woven through these pages.

To my family, who believed in the urgency of this message with me, and prayed as I wept in secret. You helped carry the burden. You are pillars in the storm.

To the watchmen and remnant voices across the world who refuse to compromise: You inspired this cry. You confirmed its timing. This book carries your tears, your boldness, and your midnight oil.

To my fellow writers, theologians, and friends—thank you for sharpening the vision and challenging the call with love and truth. The Kingdom of God is better because of you.

To the Church, both bruised and beautiful—this is for you. May your lamp be filled. May your veil be ready. May your eyes be fixed on the eastern sky.

And finally, to every reader, thank you for taking this journey with me to the edge of the world's final chapter. May this book wake you. Stir you. Send you.

For the trumpet is not a metaphor.
It is the sound of reality approaching.
Let him that hath ears hear.
With deepest honor and reverence,

—Damiano B. Centola
Los Angeles, California

About the Author

Damiano B. Centola is a prophetic author, visionary theologian, and Spirit-led messenger for this generation. With a body of work that spans sacred geometry, biblical prophecy, spiritual devotion, and divine mysteries, his writings ignite hearts with urgency, clarity, and eternal perspective. Damiano is known for his uncompromising pursuit of truth, his reverence for Scripture, and his call to awaken the remnant Church before the return of the King.

He has authored more than thirty books, including The Mystery of Mysteries: Decoding the Divine Proportions of the Human Body Through Art, Anatomy, and Sacred Geometry, God's Sovereignty: Exploring the Divine Rule Over Creation, History, and Eternity, and Bloodline: The Battle for Divine DNA — From Eve to Mary, From Heaven to Earth — The Blood Satan Couldn't Steal. His works have touched readers across nations, blending deep theological insight with poetic power.

Damiano carries the heartbeat of the Bridegroom and speaks with the urgency of a watchman on the wall. His life's mission is to prepare the Church for the soon-coming King, to awaken the sleeping, and to echo the cry of heaven in this final hour: "Behold, He comes!"

He resides between global book tours and quiet time with God, committed to lifting up the name of Jesus with every breath, every word, and every work.

Back Cover Blurb

The trumpet is sounding... but is the Church still asleep?

In The Last Trumpet: Christ's Return and the Awakening of a Sleeping Church, prophetic author Damiano B. Centola issues a bold, Spirit-filled call to the Body of Christ in the final hour. This is not a book about timelines or theories. It is a cry from the heart of heaven — a clarion warning to the remnant, a wake-up call to the slumbering Bride, and a plea for urgent return to holiness, truth, and fire before the sky splits open.

Drawing from Scripture, typology, prophetic vision, and the condition of today's Church, this book unfolds ten powerful chapters that expose false glory, reveal the cry of the faithful remnant, and prepare the reader for the fiery return of the King. From the garden of Gethsemane to the gates of the New Jerusalem, each page confronts, convicts, and calls forth readiness.

The hour is late. The cry is clear. The return of Christ is not a theory — it is a promise.

Will you be ready when the heavens roar?

www.ingramcontent.com/pod-product-compliance
Lightning Source LLC
Chambersburg PA
CBHW061223070526
44584CB00029B/3964